D1358263

WITHDRAWN

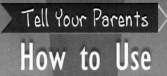

How to Use

WIND

POWER

to Light and Heat Your Home

Claire O'Neal

Mitchell Lane

P.O. Box 196
Hockessin, Delaware 19707
Visit us on the web: www.mitchelllane.com
Comments? email us: mitchelllane@mitchelllane.com

All About Electric and Hybrid Cars
Green Changes You Can Make Around Your Home
How to Harness Solar Power for Your Home
How to Use Wind Power to Light and Heat Your Home
How You Can Use Waste Energy to Heat
and Light Your Home

Special thanks to Katie Cutler and Jerome
Middle School Rotor Club kids for the use of
their photographs.

Printing   1   2   3   4   5   6   7   8   9

**Library of Congress Cataloging-in-Publication
Data**

O'Neal, Claire.
  How to use wind power to light and heat your
home / by Claire O'Neal.
     p. cm. — (Tell your parents)
  Includes bibliographical references and index.
  ISBN 978-1-58415-762-5 (library bound)
  1. Wind power—Juvenile literature.
2. Renewable energy sources—Juvenile
literature. I. Title.
  TJ820.O484 2009
  621.31'2136—dc22
                                        2009004530

                                        PLB

CONTENTS

Words in **bold** type can be found in the glossary.

Have you ever been outside in a strong storm? If so, you've felt the wind whip your clothes or maybe turn your umbrella inside out. On TV, you've probably seen the devastation that high winds from tornadoes and hurricanes can cause. That kind of wind gets a lot of bad publicity. But if wind has the power to move things, it can also do work. In fact, we can use the force of the wind to make electricity. If we could harness the wind power around the globe to work for us, we could use that energy to provide five times more electricity than the entire world needs. U.S. wind experts calculate that the possible wind power in just North Dakota, South Dakota, and Texas could provide enough electricity for the entire United States.

Scientists know that wind power is underused. In 2006, wind power generated less than one percent of the energy

A rural wind farm

A small windmill pumps water for a farm

needed to power homes in the United States. But the winds of change are blowing through the energy market, and wind power is quickly becoming big business. Wind has always been popular in Europe. Denmark, Spain, Portugal, and Germany are world leaders in wind technology. The United States has been slow to catch up, but during 2008 alone, the wind power supplied by the United States doubled. The U.S. Department of Energy has set a goal to generate 20 percent of all U.S. electricity using wind by 2030. Other countries around the world are doing the same.

Electricity from wind power has obvious benefits. The wind will continue to blow every day, making wind power a reliable, **renewable energy** source. Wind power also generates no pollution or toxic waste. However, modern wind power is a

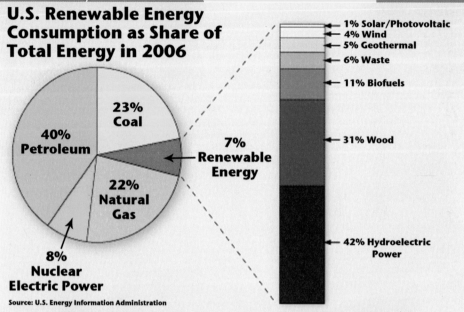

U.S. Renewable Energy Consumption as Share of Total Energy in 2006

- 1% Solar/Photovoltaic
- 4% Wind
- 5% Geothermal
- 6% Waste
- 11% Biofuels
- 31% Wood
- 42% Hydroelectric Power

40% Petroleum

23% Coal

22% Natural Gas

8% Nuclear Electric Power

7% Renewable Energy

Source: U.S. Energy Information Administration

The U.S. runs mostly on nonrenewable energy sources, which met 93% of energy needs in 2006. Wind power and other renewable energy sources are seriously underused.

relatively new and expensive technology. To save money, most of the world's electricity is produced by burning **fossil fuels**, such as coal, oil, or natural gas. Fossil fuels are a **nonrenewable energy** source, created within the earth over millions of years. Our society depends heavily on cheap and abundant energy from fossil fuels, but our dependence on these fuels has serious consequences.

Fossil fuels are responsible for a shocking amount of pollution on the ground and in the sky. Burning fossil fuels causes smog and acid rain, and it releases many toxic compounds into the air, including ash, **radioactive** elements, and mercury. Burning fossil fuels also releases greenhouse gases such as carbon dioxide, methane, and nitrous oxide. Levels of these gases have increased greatly since the 1700s, when people began to burn coal in factories. Because high amounts of greenhouse gases raise the temperature of the earth, the Intergovernmental Panel on Climate Change (IPCC) blames our use of fossil fuels for recent trends in global warming. The IPCC reported in 2001 that if global warming continues, it will melt enough ice in icebergs and at the poles to raise the global sea level. Islands and major cities near oceans could become permanently flooded.

It is easy to downplay the environmental effects of using fossil fuels when they are so cheap and easy to come by. But they will not always be, nor have they been in the past. In fact, since about the year 2000, the price of oil has been

Power plants that burn fossil fuels spew chemicals into the air, including greenhouse gases and the ingredients for smog and acid rain.

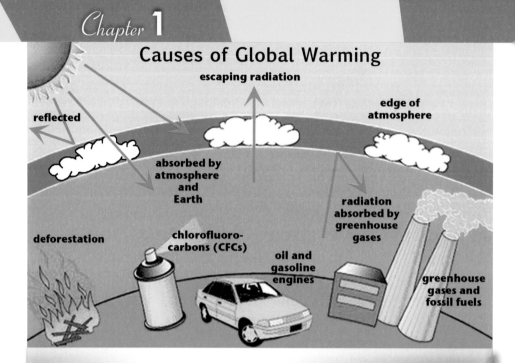

Causes of Global Warming

escaping radiation

edge of atmosphere

reflected

absorbed by atmosphere and Earth

radiation absorbed by greenhouse gases

deforestation

chlorofluoro-carbons (CFCs)

oil and gasoline engines

greenhouse gases and fossil fuels

Natural compounds like carbon dioxide and artificial chemicals like chlorofluorocarbons (CFCs) are examples of greenhouse gases, which trap the sun's energy and heat the earth. Burning fossil fuels releases extra carbon dioxide into the atmosphere. Trees could use this carbon dioxide, but people continue to cut down or burn whole forests. Only recently has society begun to understand that greenhouse gases may cause global warming.

unpredictable. It rose to a record high price—$147.30 per barrel—in July 2008. By February 2009, the price had dropped to about $36.00 per barrel.

Cheap oil is of serious importance to the U.S. economy, because gasoline comes from oil. Americans tend to live far from where they work, and to buy food and goods that are transported to stores over long distances. The cars that take workers to their jobs and the trucks that bring the things we buy use a large supply of gas every day. The United States alone uses over 20 million barrels of oil daily. Though coal is a power plant favorite, because our society depends so heavily on cars, the United States gets more of its energy from oil than from any other source.

Because oil and coal are nonrenewable, there will come a time when there is no more supply, no more to pump or to mine. No one knows for sure how much fossil fuel is left in the earth, but scientists at the U.S. Geological Survey have predicted that the world oil supply could dry up as early as 2075. Scientist Gregson Vaux predicts that the world's coal may be used up by 2110.

When coal and oil are gone, will another form of energy be ready to take their place? The current energy **infrastructure**—the systems and machines that produce and transport energy—depends so strongly on coal and oil that more costly alternatives have been pushed out, not explored and not developed. If coal and oil ran out immediately, the world would be plunged into an energy crisis. There would be little energy to run cars, trains, buses, or airplanes. Most houses would not have lights at night, or heat or air conditioning. Clean water would run out if the city couldn't use electricity to purify or pump it. If we don't find alternatives to fossil fuel power, we may soon be left with no power at all.

What can you do to make a difference? The fastest and easiest way is to try to conserve energy around your house. The average U.S. resident uses more electricity than anyone else in the world. But what if you want to do more to reduce pollution and to help find an answer to our energy problems? Read on to find out if wind power may be an answer for your family. Not everyone lives in a place where wind power is available or even practical. But if those who do take advantage of the clean energy that wind has to offer, Earth will have a brighter future.

An Egyptian seagoing ship

HISTORY OF WIND POWER

For thousands of years, people have used wind to ease their workload. One of the first inventions to use wind to do work was the sail. The first evidence of sails comes from pottery paintings made by ancient Egyptians around 3500 BCE. Before boats had sails, they were rowed. Larger boats like warships could only move around with the help of huge populations of slaves. Sails not only freed slaves from the galleys, they also allowed the ships' masters to travel farther than ever before. Using sail-powered ships, ancient peoples could expand their countries by exploring new territory. They could trade goods with faraway lands—or conquer them.

The next major wind-powered advance was the windmill, which was first documented in what is now France in 1180 CE. Old windmills were flat wooden boards attached to a

Tourists visit an ancient windmill

In Cervantes' novel, Don Quixote imagines windmills as vicious giants

central spoke. When the force of the wind pushed the boards, the spoke turned. The spoke was attached to something that could do useful work, such as a pump to bring water from a well or out of a lake, a heavy stone to grind grain, or a saw to cut wood. Before windmills, farmers would pump water from their wells themselves, while their wives spent long hours grinding grain by hand. As historian Edward Kealey wrote in his book *Harvesting the Air*, the "windmill was above all a triumph of ingenuity over toil."

The windmill also brought social change. Poor farmers no longer depended on water-powered mills, which were often controlled by landowners or churches who charged fees for grinding grain. Rivers and creeks that could be dammed to run water-powered mills were in short supply, but wind was everywhere and could be used by anyone. By the 1600s, windmills were so widespread over the landscape of Europe and China that they were often featured in paintings and novels. In one famous story, *Don Quixote* (kee-HOH-tee) by Spanish author Miguel Cervantes (ser-VAHN-teez), the hero attacks a windmill when he mistakes it for an enemy.

The image of the Dutch windmill is common even today, because windmills revolutionized life in the Netherlands starting in the 1600s. Much of the Netherlands is below sea level, and many villages are built in **polders**, or low-lying land surrounded by walls called **dykes** that keep out the water. For hundreds of years, the Dutch lost crops and even whole villages due to flooding when dykes and drainage systems

The village of Kinderdijk, Netherlands, lies in a polder. Dutch engineers built nineteen windmills around 1740 CE to pump out water and keep the town dry. Tourists from all over the world still visit the original windmills, which the United Nations has named a World Heritage Site.

failed. In the seventeenth century, water levels in Lake Haarlemmermeer rose and threatened to drown parts of Amsterdam. Dutch engineer Jan Leeghwater organized a system of windmills to drain it. Today a village, an airport, and several train stations stand in a polder where Lake Haarlemmermeer was, and one of Leeghwater's original pumping stations still keeps the polder dry. The Dutch continue to use windmills to reclaim wetlands to shape their country as they wish. A famous Dutch saying goes, "God created the world, but the Dutch created Holland."

In the 1880s, British professor James Blyth became the first in the world to use wind power for electricity. In the garden of his vacation home in Marykirk, Scotland, Blyth built a tower 33 feet high and attached cloth sails to make a **turbine**. The turbine charged a battery that stored the electricity and powered the house's lights. Blyth's experiment was so successful that he made more power than he could use. But when he offered the extra electricity to the city, the people of the town refused, saying his wind power was "the work of the devil." In the 1890s, Danish scientist and high school teacher Poul la Cour invented a wind-powered system that supplied electricity to his school for seven years.

Like wind, electricity is a natural force. Benjamin Franklin realized this in 1752, when he famously flew a kite during a lightning storm and watched sparks jump to his hand from a metal key tied to the kite string. However, no one really gave much thought to using electricity in a practical way until the nineteenth century. In 1800, Alessandro Volta invented the first battery, a way to store electricity. Called the "voltaic pile," it had alternating layers of zinc and copper. Volta also showed that electricity could travel through wires. In September 1820, Danish scientist Hans Christian Oersted and French scientist Andre-Marie Ampère discovered that magnets could

Danish teacher and engineer Poul la Cour built these two turbines at Askov Folk High School in Denmark. His first turbine (on the right) was built in 1891.

affect, and even create, electricity. In 1821, British scientist Michael Faraday found that, by rotating a magnet inside a coil of wire, he could generate an electric current. Faraday was the first to make usable electricity.

In modern times, most of our electricity comes from power plants that use generators much like Michael Faraday's. These generators are much larger and use electromagnets instead of natural magnets to produce a stronger magnetic field. Instead of a simple coil of wire, these enormous generators use miles and miles of copper wire. The electromagnet is mounted on a shaft, which is attached to a turbine. Most power plants turn the turbine using the pushing power of steam. The steam turns the turbine, which turns the shaft, which generates a magnetic field in the generator and causes electricity to flow.

Electricity is a kind of *power,* the scientific term for energy used or made over a period of time. Just as we can measure length or temperature, we can measure power. Scientists measure power in **watts**, but one watt by itself doesn't provide much useful electrical power. It takes 60 watts to power a common lightbulb for an hour. Power utilities usually measure household use in **kilowatt-hours** (kWh). It takes one thousand watts to make a kilowatt. The average home in the U.S. uses 920 kWh per month. To service thousands of customers, a power plant makes millions of watts, or megawatts (MW), of energy. The largest power plant in the world, Three Gorges Dam in China, can produce 10 million MW per month.

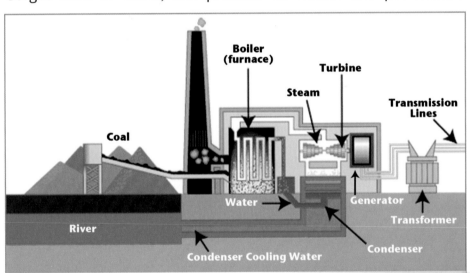

Power plants generate electricity by spinning an electromagnet, usually attached to a turbine (right), inside a large coil of copper wire. Many power plants burn coal in a huge furnace to boil water, and then steam pushes the turbine's blades. Hydroelectric power plants use flowing water to push the blades; wind farms use wind.

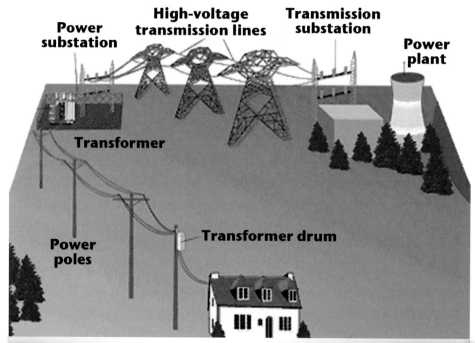

Power substation
High-voltage transmission lines
Transmission substation
Power plant
Transformer
Transformer drum
Power poles

The power grid delivers electricity from a power plant to your home. Power plants output alternating current (AC) electricity, which can travel long distances with little loss in power by adjusting its voltage. A substation near the power plant ramps up the voltage, while another one near your neighborhood decreases the voltage to a level your house can handle.

Power plants use one of many different sources to provide enough heat to make the steam required to turn the generator. The most common sources are petroleum, coal, or natural gas, which are burned in huge furnaces. In nuclear power plants, heat is released when unstable elements, such as uranium or plutonium, break down. Nuclear power doesn't pollute the air, but it does generate solid radioactive waste that is poisonous to living things. In biomass power plants, water is heated when dead plants and **organic** trash is burned. Waste-to-energy plants burn all kinds of household trash. Biomass and household trash are considered renewable

As early as 500 to 900 CE, Persians may have developed a unique windmill independently of the rest of the world. Their version of the windmill rotated around a vertical axis and was used to pump water and grind grain.

forms of energy, but burning trash certainly creates air pollution. Clean, renewable **geothermal** energy power plants use heat from the earth, though this resource is only available in areas with geysers, hot springs, or volcanoes. Iceland and the Philippines use geothermal energy to generate much of their electricity.

Hydroelectric power and wind power, however, are completely different. These methods skip the water-boiling step entirely. Hydro- and wind power both generate electricity directly by forcing a fluid—water or wind—through a turbine attached to a generator. Though they are the oldest technologies, water and wind power remain important on the energy scene. Hydroelectric power stations sit on rivers, whose water is channeled through turbines inside large dams. Seven of the top ten largest power plants in the world use hydropower. Wind power stations, called **wind farms,** are collections of turbines placed on a windy site. Wind farms can supply large amounts of clean electricity, and in more possible locations than hydro and geothermal energy. The potential of wind power has scientists and governments excited around the world.

Francis Turbine is 34 feet across and generates power at the Three Gorges Dam Power Plant in China.

八 局
轮顺利吊入厂房

Nysted Wind Farm

HOW DOES WIND POWER WORK?

Just off the coast of Denmark, a country surrounded by ocean, engineers use the constant wind to make electricity. They do this with enormous wind turbines, each around 100 feet across. Turbines are state-of-the-art windmills, designed for efficiency and durability. Wind turbines look a lot like fans, but in many ways they are opposites. Fans around your house use electricity to create wind. Wind turbines use wind to create electricity.

Denmark pioneered the strategy to build enormous offshore wind farms, transporting the electricity back to land through wires buried in the seabed. Their latest project, the Nysted Wind Farm, was completed in 2003. It is the second largest wind farm in the world, with 72 wind turbines that produce nearly 600,000 megawatts of electricity per year. They supply

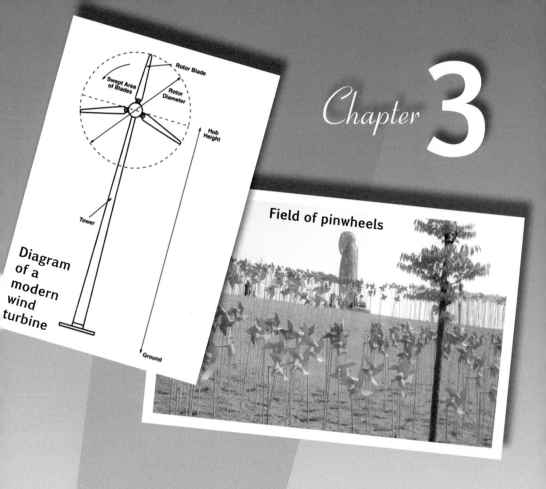

Diagram of a modern wind turbine

Swept Area of Blades
Rotor Blade
Rotor Diameter
Hub Height
Tower
Ground

Field of pinwheels

power to 145,000 Danish homes. Overall, wind provides 19 percent of Denmark's electricity, making this small country the world leader in wind power.

Denmark uses its natural geography to its advantage; its many miles of coastline help ensure strong winds. Coastal winds are strong because of the large difference in temperature between the land and the ocean. When the sun heats one area of the earth's surface, such as the land, the air above it also gets hot and rises. Then cooler air, such as that above the ocean, moves in from an area close by to replace it. Wind is the horizontal part of this movement. The greater the temperature difference between two areas, the greater the movement of air, and the faster the wind will blow. This is true everywhere. Strong winds are felt not just at coastlines,

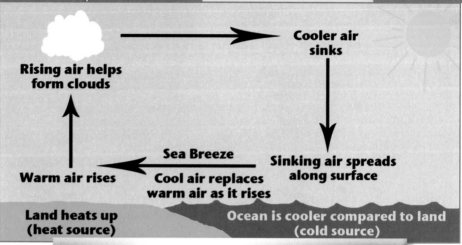

Rising air helps form clouds

Cooler air sinks

Warm air rises

Sea Breeze
Cool air replaces warm air as it rises

Sinking air spreads along surface

Land heats up (heat source)

Ocean is cooler compared to land (cold source)

Wind is formed when hot surfaces heat the air above them, making the air rise. Cooler air rushes in to fill that empty space, creating wind.

but also along mountain ranges, prairies, and other places where the sun heats the earth's surface unevenly.

Wind turbines make electricity the same way a power plant does, only on a smaller scale. The turbine's blades attach at a central point, called the hub, and the hub and blades together are called the **rotor**. When the rotor turns, it spins a shaft. The rotating shaft is part of an **alternator**. When the shaft spins, it creates a magnetic field that produces electricity in the alternator's wires. The electricity flows along wires that carry it to its final destination, a **power grid** or a house (see page 16). If the turbine is connected to a battery, the electricity can charge the battery and be stored for later use.

Modern wind turbines are specially engineered to transfer the most power possible from blowing wind to the alternator. Modern turbine blades are shaped to catch the fullest possible force of the wind. They are usually made of fiberglass, which is light and durable. Most turbines have three solid blades,

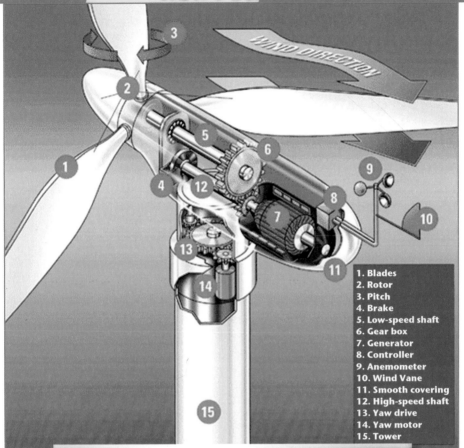

1. Blades
2. Rotor
3. Pitch
4. Brake
5. Low-speed shaft
6. Gear box
7. Generator
8. Controller
9. Anemometer
10. Wind Vane
11. Smooth covering
12. High-speed shaft
13. Yaw drive
14. Yaw motor
15. Tower

A wind turbine rotor contains specialized parts that help it turn into the wind and stay level, protect it from high-speed winds, and generate electricity.

the fewest needed to balance the rotor as it turns about its shaft.

The rotor also needs to be able to turn from side to side to cope with changing wind direction. Small turbines have a tail fin that quickly steers the blades into the wind. However, large wind turbines—like those found on wind farms—are too big to move this way. These sophisticated machines use

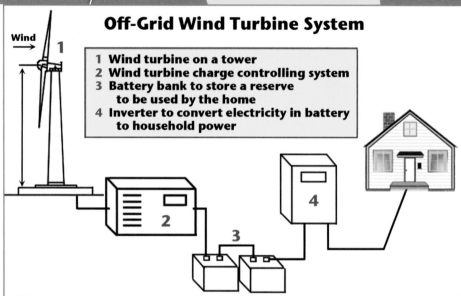

Off-Grid Wind Turbine System

Wind →

1 Wind turbine on a tower
2 Wind turbine charge controlling system
3 Battery bank to store a reserve
   to be used by the home
4 Inverter to convert electricity in battery
   to household power

There are two major types of "small wind" systems for your home—off-grid and grid-tie. An off-grid system relies on the turbine (1) for all electricity, because no other power lines are connected to the house. The wind turbine outputs electricity to a battery (3), where it is stored until it is needed.

onboard weather sensors to detect changes in wind direction. The sensors control motors that turn the rotor into the wind. When the wind becomes too strong, like in a storm, the rotor may spin too fast and damage the turbine. Most systems have an automatic safety shut-off. They also have a limiter that slows the rotor to a safe speed.

Household-sized wind turbines require additional parts to deliver electricity to homes. The electricity a wind turbine creates is not exactly like the electricity that comes out of a standard wall outlet, which in the United States always measures 60 **Hertz** (frequency) and 120 **volts**. Wind turbines generate "wild" alternating current, which varies in voltage and frequency. This is because the rotor creating the electricity

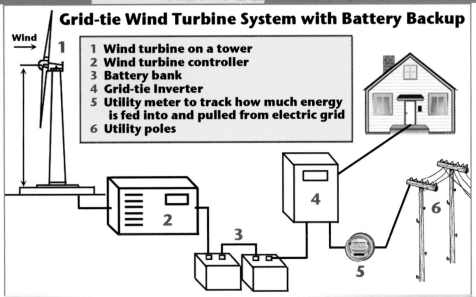

Grid-tie Wind Turbine System with Battery Backup

Wind →

1

1 **Wind turbine on a tower**
2 **Wind turbine controller**
3 **Battery bank**
4 **Grid-tie Inverter**
5 **Utility meter to track how much energy is fed into and pulled from electric grid**
6 **Utility poles**

In a grid-tie system, the turbine's electricity taps into the same wires as the power company. The turbine (1) provides electricity to the house or to the power grid whenever the wind is blowing. Though you can have a battery backup (3), most people don't, so on less windy days the house uses electricity from the power grid (6).

does not spin at the same frequency all the time. A controller in the turbine converts "wild" alternating current (AC) to direct current (DC). An inverter then converts the DC into standard AC and sends the electricity into the home. The inverter connects to the same wires the power company uses, making home wind power convenient to install.

There are several factors that affect the energy-making capability, or **capacity,** of a turbine. One is its size. Longer blades catch more wind and generate more electricity. The smallest turbines, at 5 feet in diameter, supply only enough power to charge a car battery. That may not seem like a lot, but these small wind structures have brought big changes to remote areas all over the world. They are common sights

The largest wind farm in the world is in Altamont Pass, California, an hour's drive from San Francisco. It is also one of the oldest. Since construction began in 1980, over 4,900 turbines have been installed there.

in developing countries in Africa and Asia, where they can pump enough water from a well to serve the needs of a whole village or a farm of livestock. Wind customers in industrialized countries, however, will need something bigger. The turbine manufacturer Aerostar calculates that a very efficient turbine with a diameter of 6 feet should produce 90 kilowatts (kW) per month in 12-mile-per-hour winds—enough to power a television set. In the same conditions, a 12-foot-diameter rotor will output 361 kW per month, enough to power a television set, a lightbulb, and a computer. By doubling the rotor diameter, you quadruple (multiply by 4) the system's capacity. Turbines used in wind farms produce up to 2.5 MW under the same conditions. Their 300-foot-diameter rotors are as long as a football field!

No matter what a turbine's size, unless it is mounted in the right location, it will not perform at its best. The site of a turbine installation is researched carefully to make sure the turbine will receive the most wind possible. Wind engineers look at weather reports and wind power maps to find places with the fastest winds. Then, they mount the turbine on a tower high above the ground in those places. Wind speed increases as you rise above the earth. For example, if the wind speed is 20 miles per hour (mph) at 30 feet off the ground, it will be 26 mph at 120 feet. Though that may not seem like a big change, turbines produce energy more efficiently at higher speeds. A turbine mounted at 120 feet will produce almost twice as much power as it would at 30 feet. Because of this, an essential part of a wind turbine is its tower. Wind engineers maximize energy production by mounting turbines on the tallest towers possible. Towers that support industrial turbines stand 400 feet or taller!

There are many factors to consider when building and installing a wind turbine. With careful planning, a single turbine can produce abundant, clean energy for twenty years or more.

Rooftop wind turbine

"SMALL WIND" AND YOU

Wind power is the cheapest of all green energy to buy and install on your own property. The American Wind Energy Association states that the average "small wind" home installation costs $32,000. In contrast, to install solar panels on a typical house costs over $50,000. While this may seem expensive, the government rewards efforts to use clean energy with tax breaks and grants. For example, many states give homeowners at least half the cost of a new wind turbine installation. Keep in mind, too, that a properly installed wind turbine should last twenty years or more. Because the turbine will make most of your electricity, it will probably pay for itself over time in lower electric bills. What's more, most home wind turbines are connected to the power grid. If you make more electricity than you use, the utility pays you for

A wind turbine in motion

the extra power. If you live in a really windy place, you may end up making a profit.

To determine what size turbine is right for your family, first you need to know how much electricity you use per month. Keep an eye on your electric bill, which will report your household use in kilowatt-hours. The amount may shock you!

Before you begin shopping, all wind turbine manufacturers recommend you first change your habits to minimize your family's electricity use at home. Household wind turbines are overwhelmed by the typical American family's energy usage. Can you think of ways you can use less electricity? You'd be surprised how easy it is to make little changes around the house that add up quickly. You probably know to turn off lights when you leave the room. If you replace your lightbulbs

Electric Meter Information

Meter Number 9CAMR674

Current Meter Reading, Mar 23 (actual)	013571
Last Meter Reading, Feb 23 (actual)	012503
Total KWHs Used	1068

Your Next Scheduled Meter Reading is Apr 22, 2009

Electric Charges

Current charges for 28 days - Winter Rates in Effect - Residential Service

For Account 3479 8219 9999, the class average annual price to compare is 11.96 cents per kWh
  Delivery Charges:

Customer Charge	$	7.36
Distribution Charge: First 500 kWh X $0.023460 Each kWh	$	11.73
Last 568 kWh X $0.023460 Each kWh	$	13.32
Total Electric Delivery Charges	$	**32.41**
Total Electric Charges	$	**32.41**

Your Electric Energy Comparison

Daily Averages:

	Mar 08	Mar 09
Temp:	43°	40°
KWH:	36.1	38.1

Letters above graph
denote reading type
A - Actual
E - Estimated
C - Corrected
U - Customer

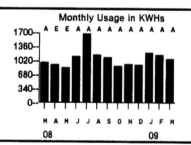

Monthly Usage in KWHs

Electric Supply Summary - WGES

Delmarva Power Account 3479 8219 9999

Supplier Account
Current Charges for 28 days - Residential Service
1068 KWHs Used

Billing Period:
from: Feb 23, 2009
to: Mar 23, 2009

Electric Supply Summary - WGES

Remaining Balance as of Mar 25	$	0.00
Total Use: 1068kwh at $0.119 per kwh	127.09	
Total Current Charges	$	127.09
Total Energy Charge	$	127.09

This customer's electricity comes from a wind power supplier (WGES). She used 1068 kWh (top) during March 2009, or about 38 kWh each day (middle). Last March she used a little less energy, about 36 kWh a day. The bar graph shows a spike in electricity use in July 2008, when her refrigerator was not working properly.

with energy-efficient fluorescent ones, you'll use even less electricity when the lights are on.

Your thermostat controls your furnace and air conditioner, the two biggest drains on your energy budget. Save a lot by keeping your thermostat set warmer in the summer and cooler in the winter. Programmable thermostats will adjust the temperature automatically at certain times of the day, which will save even more energy. Hang your laundry out to dry when you can instead of using the dryer. And your refrigerator will use less electricity if you vacuum the coils regularly on the back and underneath—and if you keep the door closed while you're pouring something to drink.

After reducing your family's electricity needs, you may find that you can save money and get a smaller turbine. Even if you decide not to go "small wind," you'll be using less electricity and making a positive impact on the environment. Your parents will appreciate their lower energy bills, too!

Next, you need to know the average wind speed in your area to determine a turbine's capacity. You can find this information online—just check the weather forecast or the web site of a local airport.

Time to shop for a turbine! Turbines come with labels called nameplate ratings. This naming system describes how much electricity—10 kW, 25 kW, etc.—the turbine produces in a certain wind speed. Unfortunately, the wind speed and label are chosen by the manufacturer, meaning you can't use the nameplates to compare two brands or even to match a turbine to your electricity needs. Instead, look for brochures that list the monthly or annual electricity output at different wind speeds, matching the model's output to the average wind speed found in your area.

Your parents may not be willing to pay enough to cover all your family's electricity needs with a turbine, but any of

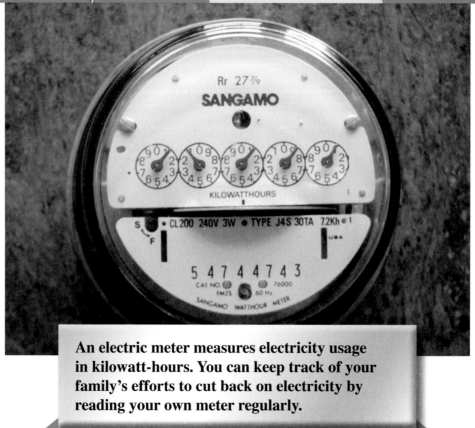

An electric meter measures electricity usage in kilowatt-hours. You can keep track of your family's efforts to cut back on electricity by reading your own meter regularly.

a number of affordable models could certainly make a dent in your electricity bill. In making the final selection, Mick Sagrillo, wind expert and owner of Sagrillo Power and Light in Forestville, Wisconsin, recommends you look for a good **warranty** and stick to a trusted name brand (such as ARE, Aerostar, Bergey, Jacobs, Proven, or Vestas), or at least to a well-known and proven turbine model. Don't forget necessary extras that add to the cost, such as a tower and professional installation. When your parents decide, they can order their system by mail, over the phone, or, for some models, even online.

Wind power is an exciting technology, but it's important to know that small wind is not practical for everyone. To make enough electricity to be useful, wind turbines must be placed in a location where the average wind speed is 9 mph or higher. Rotors on modern turbines will not turn at all until the wind reaches around 7 mph. Much of the country, especially the southeast and the desert southwest, are simply not windy enough to make wind power cost-efficient.

Land is an additional requirement for the small wind owner. Wind companies recommend installing household-sized turbines at least 30 feet above anything that can stop the wind, such as buildings or trees. A tower like that requires open land. Farms are perfect candidates for wind installations,

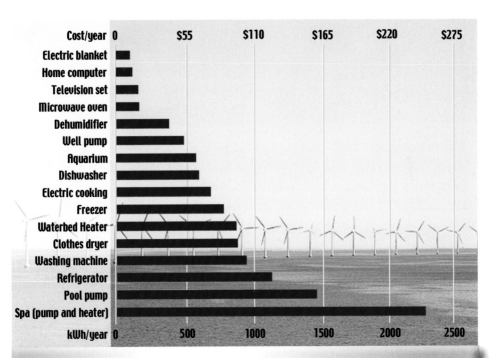

Cost/year	0	$55	$110	$165	$220	$275
Electric blanket						
Home computer						
Television set						
Microwave oven						
Dehumidifier						
Well pump						
Aquarium						
Dishwasher						
Electric cooking						
Freezer						
Waterbed Heater						
Clothes dryer						
Washing machine						
Refrigerator						
Pool pump						
Spa (pump and heater)						
kWh/year	0	500	1000	1500	2000	2500

How much electricity do your appliances use every year? Look along the bottom of the chart to find out. Remember that using electricity costs money. Values along the top of the chart tell you how much, based on a rate of 11 cents per kilowatt-hour. Your rate may be higher or lower, depending on where you live.

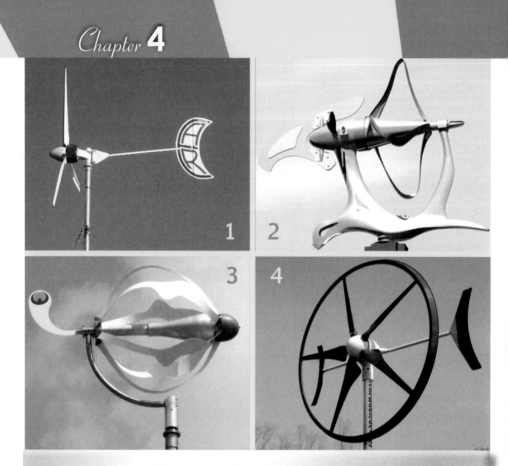

There are many different models of home wind turbines, including these four: 1) the ARE110 by Abundant Renewable Energy; 2) the Loopwing by Loopwing Company; 3) the Energy Ball V100 by Home Energy; 4) Swift wind turbine by Cascade Engineering.

but anyone with an acre or more can build a 60-foot-tall tower. Unfortunately, that rules out small wind for apartment dwellers or families with small yards. And even if your family has enough land, some areas have laws against building structures that tall. Be sure to check with the local building inspector in your city government office to find out what the rules are.

As gung-ho as you may be about wind power, you should probably also ask your neighbors before you proceed. When running, home turbines register at about 50 decibels, or about as loud as a refrigerator. While this is not extremely loud, most people can certainly hear them. If your neighbors don't like the noise, they are more likely to complain about how the turbine looks. In the United States, a major drawback for some wind farms is that not everyone wants to see a landscape covered with towers. A famous wind farm that has

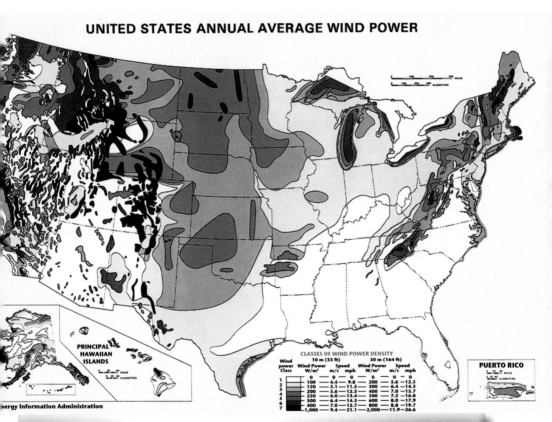

UNITED STATES ANNUAL AVERAGE WIND POWER

PRINCIPAL HAWAIIAN ISLANDS

PUERTO RICO

ergy Information Administration

This map color-codes the U.S. based on local wind speeds, with white areas (class 1) being the least windy and the navy blue areas (class 7) the most windy. Home wind turbines work best in wind power class areas 3 to 7. As turbine technology improves, home turbines may become practical just about everywhere.

met with overwhelming resistance is the Cape Wind project off Nantucket, Massachusetts. Engineers picture this large wind farm of 130 turbines, each 440 feet tall, installed 5 miles offshore in the waters of Nantucket Sound. The wind farm would produce up to 420 MW of electricity per day for residents of the sound and surrounding islands. However, residents feel it would destroy

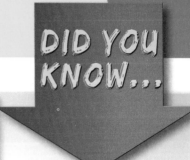

DID YOU KNOW...

The fastest wind speed ever measured that wasn't a tornado occurred on April 12, 1934, when a 231-mph gust blasted Mount Washington, New Hampshire.

the classic views of the Atlantic Ocean enjoyed by their community for over 300 years. They are also concerned with how ocean life will tolerate the construction and operation of such a large installation, and how the towers will affect navigation through the sound for fishermen. Though your neighbors probably won't complain about such things with your home wind turbine, they are important issues for governments to consider.

The most important drawback to wind power is that a turbine cannot make electricity unless the wind is blowing. During windless times, you will have to buy electricity from the power company. Also, unless you have a battery, the extra energy made during really windy times cannot be stored. Turbine installations are typically wired so that the electricity made is either used immediately or transferred to the grid. Families interested in living off the grid may want to consider buying batteries for emergency backup, or adding solar panels to their home to pick up the slack on windless days.

Wind power has definite pros and cons. If you live in a windy place with a lot of land, wind power may be just right

Wind turbines and solar panels complement each other well. With both, you may not need a battery backup to live off the grid.

for you. If you don't live in a windy place, you may still be able to take advantage of wind power. Power companies everywhere are responding to customers' demand for cleaner energy. For a little extra money per kilowatt-hour, your utility company may allow customers to purchase green energy from wind farms or from other renewable sources, such as hydroelectric, solar, or geothermal power stations. It may cost more, but you can feel proud that you're doing your part to support energy alternatives for the future.

Shattuck Windmill Museum in Shattuck, Oklahoma

SPIRIT LAKE, A "WIND-WIND" SITUATION

Craig Newell and Harold Overmann sat together on the football field and talked as they watched the kids of Spirit Lake High School play flag football. It was yet another windy day in the tiny town of Spirit Lake, northern Iowa, where games at the local high school were the place to be. Right on the Iowa Great Lakes, the residents of Spirit Lake were no strangers to high winds.

This time Newell was struck with an idea. He was a dentist, a scientist at heart. He was also the president of the school board. What if, he wondered, there was some way to put all this wind to use for the school? Overmann, the school's superintendent, encouraged Newell to look into it. Newell did just that, and he presented the information he

A convoy of turbine blades

The Magenn Power Air Rotor System

found about installing wind power to the school board in September 1992.

No school in Iowa had ever pursued the installation of a wind turbine before, and there was much to be done. The school board determined the energy needs of each school and shared their figures with different turbine manufacturers, three of which fought to take on the project. Wind World won, and sent the school a bill for $239,000 for a 250-kW wind turbine and its installation.

In the meantime, the school district quickly waded through a sea of paperwork. They paid for professional wind studies on their property to determine the best place for their turbine. They obtained the proper building permits. The toughest job was working with the public utility, Alliant Energy, who disliked losing such a valuable customer. In the end, the two parties agreed on the "net metering" system commonly used with small wind installations. On days when the turbine generated more energy than the school used, Alliant would buy the extra energy for 2 cents per kWh, then sell it to other customers on the grid. On less windy days, when the turbine couldn't meet the school's demand, the school would buy its electricity from Alliant, just as it had before, for 9.7 cents per kWh.

To pay for the turbine, the school applied for a grant from the U.S. Department of Energy, and received a check for half the cost of the turbine. The other half was paid for with a low-interest loan from the Iowa Department of Natural Resources. Installation began behind the elementary school playground in 1992, and the turbine began producing electricity in June 1993.

From the start, the turbine generated more energy than the elementary school could use, producing 300,000 kW per year. Instead of getting a huge electricity bill each month, the school district got a small check. With the savings and small profit, the school district paid off its 10-year loan in only 6½ years.

The school board began construction on a second, larger turbine purchased from NEG Micon for $800,000. In 2001, the 750-kW turbine began supplying power to both Spirit Lake Middle School and Spirit Lake High School, as well as to the district headquarters, the technical school, the bus garage, and the high school football field's lights. The district paid off its loan for the new turbine in 2007.

By 2009, the Spirit Lake school district was making about $8,000 each year selling extra energy back to Alliant. And because the district no longer gets a sizable electric bill, it

Spirit Lake's two wind turbines provide nearly all the electricity the school district needs. Importantly, wind power also provides jobs to rural areas like Spirit Lake, bringing opportunities in construction, engineering, and turbine maintenance.

saves an additional $120,000 each year in energy costs. With the extra money, the district has hired two extra full-time staff members and one extra part-time employee, and it has funded school programs. The district expects their annual savings to grow as electricity costs rise.

Physics teacher Jan Bolluyt jokes that, for the town and schools of Spirit Lake, the situation was not just win-win, but "wind-wind." Spirit Lake students of all ages benefit from the priceless learning experience of watching the construction and day-to-day operation of the turbines. First graders ask questions about wind power and write Curious George–style books with the answers they find. Third graders write poems about wind power and experiment with wind-powered toys. In high school math and physics classes, students use statistics

In Jerome, Idaho, middle school students helped build the wind turbine that now provides their school with clean energy.

DID YOU KNOW...

In October 2008, luxury car maker Mercedes-Benz introduced a revolutionary new racecar powered by wind and the sun. The Formula Zero Racer has a huge sail, solar panels on its body, and a wind turbine on its nose.

from the turbines for problem-solving exercises, and they build their own small generators modeled after those in the turbines. The high school government class participated in a discussion at the Iowa State Legislature about wind energy.

Bolluyt feels the turbines have rallied his community as well. "It was a reason for civic pride," he says, and what's more, "it did not cost taxpayers any money whatsoever."

The Spirit Lake project has been so successful that the U.S. government began scouting out potential new school districts that might benefit from wind power. Not everyone lives on the wind-swept prairie, but those who do are signing up for government support to help decrease pollution and create long-term energy solutions.

Try This!

Make an Anemometer

Weather professionals, airplane pilots, and, of course, potential wind power customers need to know how fast the wind is blowing. They do this with an instrument called an anemometer. It's easy to make your own anemometer, and to use it for your own wind experiments.

You'll need:

- five 3-ounce paper or plastic disposable cups (like Dixie cups)
- single-hole paper punch
- two drinking straws (not bendy ones)
- stapler
- straight pin
- pencil with an eraser
- marker

1. Punch one hole each in four of the cups, about ½ inch down from the rim. These cups will be on the outside of the rotor.
2. To make the hub, punch four evenly spaced holes about ¼ inch down from the rim of the fifth cup. Punch another hole through the center of the fifth cup's bottom.
3. Now assemble the rotor. Push one straw through the hole of an outside cup; attach it by folding the straw over and stapling it to the cup. Next, push the free end of the straw through two opposite holes in the hub cup. To finish one arm, push the straw through the hole of another outside cup. Face the second wind-catching cup in the opposite direction of the first, then staple the straw to the second cup. Repeat this step with the remaining straw and two cups.
4. Rotate the straws so that all the cups are on their sides, facing the same way around the circle. Push the straight pin through the intersection of the straws, pointing the sharp end toward the hole in the bottom of the hub cup.
5. To make the axle, push the pencil, eraser-end first, through the hole in the bottom of the hub cup. Push the straight pin into the eraser. Now your anemometer is ready to spin! Blow on a cup and watch it go. To do further wind experiments, you may want to color or mark one of the cups so that you can tell when your anemometer's rotor has spun all the way around, or made one rotation. During different wind conditions, keep track of the number of rotations your anemometer makes in one minute (RPMs). Faster wind speeds will create more RPMs.

Historical Timeline

3500 BCE	Egyptians invent sails, using wind power to move boats up the Nile River.
500–900 CE	Persians may have used windmills to pump water and grind grain.
1180 CE	The first documented windmill is built in what is now France.
1300	The Dutch begin to experiment with windmills to drain flooded areas.
1600s	Jan Leeghwater drains Lake Haarlemmermeer in the Netherlands using windmills.
1752	Benjamin Franklin better understands electricity after flying his kite in a storm.
1800	Alessandro Volta invents the first battery for storing electricity.
1800s	Americans rely on windmills to pump water as they settle the Western frontier.
1820	Hans Christian Oersted and Andre-Marie Ampère discover electromagnetism.
1821	Michael Faraday invents a dynamo, a machine that generates electric current.
1887	British professor James Blyth invents a windmill to power his vacation home in Marykirk, Scotland.
1888	American Charles Brush builds a windmill in Cleveland, Ohio.
1890s	Danish scientist and teacher Poul la Cour builds a windmill to power his school.
Early 1900s	Electric wind turbines begin to power homes throughout Europe and rural America.
1920s	G.J.M. Darrieus, a French inventor, creates a vertical-axis turbine. His design comes to be called an eggbeater turbine.
1931	Russia builds the first commercial power plant that uses a wind turbine to generate electricity.
1941	Vermont residents build a large wind turbine during a war-related energy shortage.
1971	Denmark brings the world's first offshore wind farm online.
1973	The Organization of Petroleum-Exporting Countries (OPEC) stops trading oil with several countries, including the United States, sparking widespread interest in alternative energy sources.
1980	The U.S. government begins a program that gives tax breaks to businesses that use renewable energy.
1985	In California, over 250,000 homes are powered by wind energy.
2001	World wind capacity is 24,800 MW.
2006	World wind capacity is 74,000 MW.
2007	The U.S. nearly doubles its wind power over the course of the year.
2008	World wind capacity is 94,000 MW and climbing.
2009	Wind power is estimated to generate as much power as 30.4 million tons of coal this year—enough to fill a coal train that could stretch from Washington, D.C., to central Utah.

Further Reading

Books

Benduhn, Tea. *Wind Power.* Strongsville, OH: Gareth Stevens Publishing, 2008.

Hall, Julie. *A Hot Planet Needs Cool Kids.* Bainbridge Island, WA: Green Goat Books, 2007.

Hock, Peggy. *Our Earth: Saving Energy.* New York: Scholastic, 2009.

Peterson, Christine. *Alternative Energy.* New York: Scholastic, 2004.

Peterson, Christine. *Wind Power.* New York: Scholastic, 2004.

Walker, Niki. *Generating Wind Power.* New York: Crabtree Publishing, 2007.

Works Consulted

American Wind Energy Association. http://www.awea.org/

Bolluyt, Jan, Tim Grieves, and Jim Tirevold. "Use of Wind Turbines in the Spirit Lake, Iowa, School District: A "Wind-Wind" Situation." *Kansas Science Teacher*, Spring 2006. http://www.emporia.edu/scimath/KansasScienceTeacher/KST_Vol16/WindTurbines.pdf.

Coonley, Douglas R. *Wind: Making It Work for You.* Philadelphia: The Franklin Institute Press, 1979.

Cunningham, Lloyd B. "Schools' Wind Turbines Power Learning." *USA Today*, October 20, 2008. http://www.usatoday.com/news/education/2008-10-14-schoolsinside_N.htm.

Fisher, Jeanette Joy. "Wind Energy Information: Spirit Lake Wind Project." *Environmental Psychology*, http://environmentpsychology.com/wind_energy_spirit_lake_project.htm, 2007.

Gipe, Paul. *Wind Energy Basics: A Guide to Small and Micro Wind Systems.* White River Junction, VT: Chelsea Green Publishing Company, 1999.

———. *Wind Energy Comes of Age.* New York: John Wiley & Sons, Inc., 1995.

"History of Wind Energy." *KidWind Project*, http://www.kidwind.org/lessons/BBwindenergyhistory.html.

National Renewable Energy Laboratory. *Small Wind Electric Systems: A Delaware Consumer's Guide.* Washington, D.C.: U.S. Department of Energy, 2003.

Potts, Michael. *The Independent Home.* Post Mills, VT: Chelsea Green Publishing Company, 1993.

Price, Trevor J. "James Blyth—Britain's First Modern Wind Power Pioneer." *Wind Engineering*, May 2005, Volume 29, Number 3, pp. 191–200.

Sagrillo, Mick, and Ian Woofenden. "Wind Turbine Buyer's Guide." *Home Power*, June and July 2007.

Svenvold, Mark. "Wind-Power Politics." *New York Times*, September 14, 2008, p. MM77.
http://www.nytimes.com/2008/09/14/magazine/14wind-t.html?pagewanted=1&_r=1

Wind Powering America. http://www.windpoweringamerica.gov.

Windpower Monthly News Magazine Online. http://www.wpm.co.nz.

Wood, John H., Gary R. Long, and David F. Morehouse. "Long Term World Oil Supply Scenarios." August 18, 2004.
http://www.eia.doe.gov/pub/oil_gas/petroleum/feature_articles/2004/worldoilsupply/oilsupply04.html

Woodside, Christine. *The Homeowner's Guide to Energy Independence.* Guilford, CT: The Lyons Press, 2006.

On the Internet

Abundant Renewable Energy
   http://www.abundantre.com/
An Inconvenient Truth, the website
   http://www.climatecrisis.net/
Cape Wind Project
   http://www.capewind.org/
Energy Kids' Page
   http://www.eia.doe.gov/kids/energyfacts/
Jerome Middle School Wind Turbine
   http://coen.boisestate.edu/WindEnergy/WfS/PhotoGallery/Jerome%20Middle%20School%20Wind%20Turbine/album/index.html
KidWind Project
   http://www.kidwind.org/lessons/students.html
Save Our Sound
   http://www.saveoursound.org/site/PageServer
Spirit Lake Community Schools Wind Energy
   http://www.spirit-lake.k12.ia.us/~jtirevold/bg/building.htm

Glossary

alternative energy (all-TUR-nah-tiv EN-er-jee)—Energy from sources that do not use up natural resources or harm the environment.

alternator (AL-tur-nay-tur)—An electric generator that produces alternating current (AC) electricity.

capacity (kuh-PAA-sih-tee)—The maximum amount of energy that can possibly be made.

dyke (DYK)—A barrier to keep water out.

fossil fuels—Organic material, made from dead animals and plants, that can be burned to make energy.

geothermal (jee-oh-THER-mul)—Using heat from the earth.

Hertz—A unit of frequency. In electricity, Hertz describes how long it takes alternating current (AC) electricity to complete a full cycle between maximum and minimum voltage.

infrastructure (IN-frah-struk-chur)—The behind-the-scenes facilities and systems needed for something to work properly.

kilowatt-hour (KIH-loh-wat OUR)—A unit of energy used in one hour by one kilowatt of power; it is abbreviated kWh.

nonrenewable (NON-ree-noo-uh-bul) **energy**—An energy source that, once used, cannot be replaced.

organic (or-GAN-ik)—Of natural origin, from something living.

polder (POHL-der)—An area of land below sea level, usually protected from floods by a system of dykes or walls.

power grid—The infrastructure—including transfer stations, transformers, wires, and other components—that delivers electricity from a power plant to a home or business.

radioactive (ray-dee-oh-AK-tiv)—Giving off energy due to the breakdown of chemical elements.

renewable (ree-NOO-uh-bul) **energy**—An energy source that can be replaced after it is used.

rotor (ROH-tur)—A rotating part of a machine.

turbine (TUR-byn)—A machine using a turning rotor that is powered by a fluid such as water or wind.

volt—A scientific unit to describe how much force is needed for a wire to carry an electric current.

warranty (WAH-ren-tee)—A written guarantee for a product you buy, which usually says that for a certain amount of time, the manufacturer will fix anything that goes wrong free of charge.

watt—A unit of power, which is energy over time.

wind farm—A collection of wind turbines at a windy site.

Index

About the AUTHOR

A versatile author, Claire O'Neal has published several books with Mitchell Lane, including *How You Can Use Waste Energy to Heat and Light Your Home* from this series. She holds degrees in English and Biology from Indiana University, and a Ph.D. in Chemistry from the University of Washington. After five years of living in Seattle, she gained a deep respect for greener living. Claire composts, recycles, and tries to turn out the lights when she leaves the room. She lives in Delaware with her husband, two young sons, and a fat black cat.